# "Threading My Scars Back Together"

# "Threading My Scars Back Together"

*How God's Amazing Grace and Love Is*
*Shown In A Girl's Life of Tragedies*

VERONICA RUDD ARNOLD

iUniverse, Inc.
Bloomington

# "THREADING MY SCARS BACK TOGETHER"
## HOW GOD'S AMAZING GRACE AND LOVE IS SHOWN IN A GIRL'S LIFE OF TRAGEDIES

*iUniverse books may be ordered through booksellers or by contacting:*

*iUniverse*
*1663 Liberty Drive*
*Bloomington, IN 47403*
*www.iuniverse.com*
*1-800-Authors (1-800-288-4677)*

*Because of the dynamic nature of the Internet, any web addresses or links contained in this book may have changed since publication and may no longer be valid. The views expressed in this work are solely those of the author and do not necessarily reflect the views of the publisher, and the publisher hereby disclaims any responsibility for them.*

*Any people depicted in stock imagery provided by Thinkstock are models, and such images are being used for illustrative purposes only.*
*Certain stock imagery © Thinkstock.*

*ISBN: 978-1-4620-5316-2 (sc)*
*ISBN: 978-1-4620-5323-0 (ebk)*

*Printed in the United States of America*

*iUniverse rev. date: 10/18/2011*

I'm quite certain you've heard many people say "That's my story and I'm sticking to it". Well, with this being said, I decided to put together a book entitled Threading My Scars Back Together where I could share strands of my life with my family, friends, loved ones and those who feel somewhat lost in despair. I went through a period in my life of about 5 1/2 years, where if I could only erase "the hurts" from my mind I would—but the scars have left marks of emotions from deep within me. Glancing back; it's not the path I would have chosen for my life; a such the young age of 14 years . . . how would one know these scars would be carried with me throughout the rest of my life while on this earth? So for the most part I stayed on course of a normal life; had some ups and downs; had some moments that I will always cherish. But; what could I have done differently if I could change some things in my life or if I could re-live my life, growing up as a teenager without a mother? God took my mother away to live with Him in heaven; September, 1969, it was the most crucial time in my life when I was maturing into woman-hood; and especially at the time when all "girl teenagers" need their mothers. She's been with Jesus for 42 years and I missed her then and even more as each day passes. Then it wasn't long after that that God took my father in 1977. Only then, when he passed away did I find out from one brother sharing with us all, our father had accepted Jesus Christ as his personal savior. I miss my father and what a real joy in knowing someday we'll all be together in Heaven with Jesus Christ.

I hope you enjoy this book because I write it with love in my heart. I have grown to love my Lord and to show you how Jesus has moved in my life over the years. I hope somebody out there reading this book right now can relate to some of the things I endured as a child growing up in the Appalachian Mountains of West Virginia before relocating south to Charlotte, North Carolina.

I write this book in loving memory of my father; *Clifford Vernon Rudd* and my mother, *Delores Virginia Winnings Rudd.*

*People who have impacted my life for many years to include:*

1) Pastor William (Bill) Bigham—Boger City Baptist Church, Lincolnton, NC

2) Dr. Chris Griggs—Denver Baptist Church—Denver, NC

I dedicate my writings to my Lord and Savior Jesus Christ giving Him glory for allowing me the time, strength and knowledge of compiling my thoughts together to share with one another. Just maybe there will be some people who read this book will be able to find hope and love in a lost and dying world and realize when tragic things happen in a person's life they will be able to find peace that passes all understanding by trusting in God and turning to Him who alone is able to give them peace. I hope this book will have an influence in their life because writing my thoughts and putting them down on paper have certainly been a healing process for me. God bless all who read this book . . . . by, Veronica Rudd Arnold

The Old Home Place "Snow Hill"
Painted by Delores Rudd

# Chapter 1

## *Hap-Happy on the Hill at Home*

*Yes, I'm the one; this* green eyes girl with brown hair who was born and lived in a small town in the rolling hills of West Virginia called Leivasy. Seems funny to mention this; but we all have characteristics about us we'd like to do away with; for me it's the ole distasteful, aweful, fearful, do-nothing with "cow-lick" that runs along my hairline in front of my face and second I must admit the presence of a "small forehead", oh yes that would be me!!! Good news being . . . I'm not the only one who carries these not-so-good attributes on our bodies for which we have no control over when we are born. I can tell already; you're smiling and it's all good.

Memories of my home on the hill is still etched in my mind; in fact; how does one ever erase memories of their old homeplace? I recall so many sweet things that took place; yet some bittersweet mindful things we did growing up as kids.

1

I'll share the distance from the bottom of the hill, crossing over the Leivasy bridge, rounding around the curves; counted twice; then you had to look straight up of about 1/2 mile; there sat this two story white house which I called home. Oh, such fond memories of that home and how my mother decorated it was so simple . . . from the floors covered with linoleum flooring in every room. She did have some scatter rugs around on the floor and it's all we needed beside our beds before climbing into bed at night. There were three girls that shared a bedroom and we each had our own bunk bed. The same with the three boys, they all shared the same bedroom; but each of them had their own bunk bed. It was nothing fancy; quilts on the beds that mother had made by hand, yet they kept us warm and comfy at night. Over by the oldest's girls bed was a bedside stand with a lamp which we used at night only. It used too much electricity to turn it on during the day; so we only turned the lamp on when absolute necessary. We used fans in the windows at night during the summer to keep cool because we could not afford any type of air conditioning for the house. So, while we were cooling off the house at night; we also had the real priviledge of melodies in our ears from the katydids that came bursting loud into the summer warm nights. They had quite a high pitch to them and I can remember them being somewhat annoying.

But, that sweet sombering melodies of these insects put us to sleep just about every night. Guess we all remember when black and white televisions came on the market for sale . . . well, my father bought a black and white television (and it was not in living color, as they used to advertise) when I was about 3 or 4 years old and oh, I can remember the excitement it brought to us kids when we got to watch television for the very first time. Mother most always had the ironing board in it's upright position at all times and don't think it ever was moved from the corner of the girl's bedroom because she did so much sewing and needed her arms length to the ironing board to press down the seams of the dresses as she made for us.

Back in the day, we also did not have indoor plumbing; so outside on the hillside stood an old wooden box called the "out-house" and some of you know what I'm talking about because more than likely there are are still some houses in the Appalachian Mountains throughout West Virginia, Kentucky, Tennessee, Ohio and North Carolina are still in operation . . . so winter, spring, summer and fall . . . we kept our path pretty trodden down to the ole out-house that stood on the hill. I remember opening the door to the out-house in the spring and summer months and before entering, I would look around for any kind of critters or spiders before I closed the door, knowing full well all spiders like those damp places for hide-out. I literally hated going up there and always wanted one of my older sisters to go with me. Winter months were especially bad at night when having to go out in the freezing cold, so sometimes mother would keep a metal pot somewhere closeby to avoid going out in the blizzard, taking the chance of getting our feet froze to the stones that lead up the hill. It seems there would always be a couple of inches of snow or more on the ground, especially back then we seem to have gotten more snow than we do now days, so heading to the out-house would not be anybody's dream to head that direction, believe me.

We drew water from the well that was not too far from the house. It's firmly etched in my mind as clear as a bell . . . the metal bucket that was hooked to a rope as the older brothers and sisters lowered the bucket down deep within the well to get a pale of water for cooking, washing and getting our baths every evening before nightfall. Now, years had gone by and my father had placed some underground water lines that ran to this hugh red handled pump which sat over the kitchen sink. My memory recollects the boys would prime and pump on that red hand until the water started flowing . . . . amazing enough, how this invention was going to bring water into the house was just best to suit our needs. Soon, we had enough buckets of water for all sorts of things . . . i.e. baths, dishes, etc. Now, we heated water on the woodstove for baths and washing up the dishes from the meals that mother prepared for this large family. Can one think for a minute how much work was involved with such a large family, to have as many chores to do in helping out around the house, and still have some normalcy within the family? It was called working together as a team and those who didn't want to get along would get a whipping from none other than dear old dad.

Follow me as I take you back in time (not too long ago) to some of the horrific snow drifts we would get in the winter. Sometimes the snow would get so deep around the homeplace, how in the world did we ever manage to get anything done during the winter months? Snow would get so deep that it would take days to melt and then the temperatures would drop so low at night and close to nightfall the icicles would begin to form on the back and front sides of the house. You would never want to slam the screen door at the back of the house because that would cause the icicles to drop and if not careful, they could put a real hurt on somebody. One evening; while visiting with some of the older sisters, I can remember one of them telling me, while they were coming home from school one afternoon, one of the girls had gotten off the path because the snow had gotten so deep during early morning hours and it was to no avail she had gotten lost—not quite sure how far she had went off course. Hearing the news of this; my father went looking for her and found her and brought her back to the house. Just stopping right here; I have to put things into perspective a little bit, so, can anyone honestly imagine the children growing up now days and can you imagine the children fussing about going to school in these conditions? They would not go to school today if they only realized what we had to go through and what we managed on a yearly school basis. But, looking back, I am not complaining because we really did not have it too bad. We mostly played outside practically year round (well not in the cold winter months much) just long enough to play in the snow. So, I'm guite certain mother embraced some peace and quiet around the house while we were in school or playing outside on weekends. I can hear her sweet voice calling out to all of us.... 'dinner's on the table, children come in and eat'. Ya know, I loved hearing those sweet sounds coming from a mother who loved us all the same.

Now not too far from the house that we lived in on top of the hill in Levisay; was this little small roof top mini house that was hidden back into this mound of dirt. That mound of dirt was what my father called the cellar. Now, this place was dark and cold back inside and kept a year-round temperature for the most part. That's where my father would store the potatoes for the winter months, well for that matter any other produce that needing cooling; it also went to the cellar. I can remember going up there with my father and he opened the door, I peeked inside, all I could see was a mound of potatoes which he had harvested. He was so proud and had every right.

# Chapter 2

## *Life Lessons Learned by Mother and Daddy*

Now, my father was tall in statue, had quite a thin look about him and was a coal miner by trade; yep, that terrible job that nobody wanted to mention exactly where their employment lies or the future of where ones living came from; but was still able to make a certain wage to barely feed their family and those men who were identified by the certain finery they wore for their working days . . . Aw, the big coal hats with the lights attached to the front of them, and . . . . and . . . . yes, stereotyped as the Appalachian coal-miners because after they had finished their work shift (whether it was the day shift, afternoon shift or the mid-night shift) their faces were covered with black coal dust all over them, from head to toe; their eyes black as coal and the stature of these men, all slumped over from having to bend down for their eight hour shifts in the dark side of those mountains in West

Virginia, yes I say, that was my father; and my mother was a stay-at-home-mother, accurately speaking. She was not very tall and over the years of bearing children, and as she got older and up in her years had put on some extra weight. Now in her younger years, she was a beautiful woman who carried herself very well. As the years went by, she rarely cut her hair; not by religious purposes; she just chose to wear it long and more than likely, she didn't have the money to go to the salon and have it cut. so in all intent and purposes, the hair style she sported back then in her 50's and 60's was pulled back and always up in a bun in the back of her head, her hair was thick and grey in color. She often complained of headaches because her hair was so long and heavy. She never complained about anything that I can remember other than those horrific headaches.

Not only could she sing; but she painted some of the most beautiful oil colors on canvas. As her mind wondered, many different scenes came to her and she would paint them by memory. Oh, what a lovely mother she was to be able to sit down and paint some of the prettiest oil paintings one has ever seen. My sister that now lives in the state of Kentucky gave me one of her paintings from years ago that I had framed. I had it appraised by a local Appraisal Firm and it appraised

9

for $1200 and that was years ago. It's worth more than that to me because she painted it. She called this picture that I have "Snow Hill" which one of the sisters tell me that is where they used to live years ago. She also enjoyed writing poetry and she wrote some of the most beautiful poems you've ever heard. When she passed away, my sister one year older than me got most of her poems. See, I told you she was talented in so many ways. I truly don't know how she found the time to paint and write poetry with all the children she had, but God saw a way for her to do the things that she loved to do. She was a godly woman, with much faith and everywhere she went she was telling others about Christ and how much she loves Him. She lived on faith day by day. There was not a day that went by people couldn't tell she was not a christian by her love. She not only talked it; she lived it and she loved it. I'll see you in Heaven one sweet day, mother! I've been saved and can't wait to see you there. Oh, how I absolutely miss my mother and I think all Christians eagerly await the reunions of their loved ones who have gone on before them in Heaven and must admit we will all meet again someday. Up to this point in my life, mother had never sat down with us girls and explain to us the journey one takes from living out our childhood dreams and maturing into young women.

Now my father, he sometimes would drink whiskey and beer when he got the ocassion too. Mother did not allow him to drink at home so he would buy that stuff and keep it hidden away in his truck. He was never abusive to any of the children and I never did see my father drunk. But I do know he drank and mother did not like it at all. While we were living in the white house that sat on the hillside in Leivasy, West Virginia . . . I remember mother telling one of the boys to go out there to his truck, find that whiskey bottle and pour that stuff out. That's one thing she hated the most was his drinking, but he wasn't allow to drink it around us kids. Many times, mother would pray on her knees for God to convict my father of his sins, repent, turning his heart over to God. He did, but not until after mother was killed that he gave his heart to Christ, repented and is now living in heaven.

Perhaps my father and mother stayed too busy through their years of life together; because they gave birth and raised seventeen children in all total; two of which died at birth, so I'm told, and they were so blessed by each one. So they had two sets of twins; 'a boy and a girl' and another 'boy and a boy'. Geez, this confuses the heck out of me even! Now, one of the twin boys died at birth; an older one of the sister shares with me that this twin died with the medical term; "blue baby", which means (common term for a child born cyanotic because of a congential cardiac or pulmonary defect causing incomplete oxygenation of the blood). Then I had a baby sister who was born after I was born and she also died at birth from pneumonia. She died in the arms of an older sister who now lives in the state of Kentucky. I am told by one of the older sisters; when I was born; I wasn't too old (maybe one or two weeks old) my mother gave me away to some neighbors down the road because she just could not afford to feed me and take care of me physically. I am correct to assume maybe two or three months passed by, she was so bothered by what she had done, that she went back to the folks she had gave me too; took me into her arms; thanked the man and woman for caring for me for the short period of time. In all intent and purposes, I'm glad because I would not have had the priviledge of knowing these brothers and sisters that made up this hugh family of mine.

# Chapter 3

## *All Of Us, Seven Brothers/Seven Sisters; Plus Me!*

So, surprisingly, . . . . when my sweet mother was not birthing children; she stayed active, constantly moving about taking care of the house, mending many holes in the boys pants; sewing dresses for the girls; cooking; cleaning, washing, ironing and the everyday stuff that goes along with "mothering" in the household of many. She never had much time to herself because her family required more attention on the things that were important to her. So, from day to day; when her feet hit the floor every morning, she began her day of events with the most "dreadful undertakings" of what we call hard work and I don't say that lightly, As she moved about through the day, I can remember her singing sweet, sweet old time gospel songs; and knew in my heart she must be a very happy person with much love in her heart to be singing songs like this which and not only that, it truly made up her character. She definitely had a beautiful voice and a "song in her heart", and I've heard many people say we should all have is a "song in our heart" which I think helps define who we are as a person. Mothers voice would capture a person's heart and I can still hear her singing sweet melodys of music and as far as I know; she never had anyone give her music lessons in her life. It just all came so natural for her. God gifted her with many talents and I will share them as we move along in the book. You will see what I mean and you will come to love this mother the same way I loved her could surely speak for everyone of my brothers and sisters and could get a Amen to that!

Looking at this on a different perspective; one generation of brothers and sisters had left home before I had joined this big family; so some of the older ones had already made their way into the work force; purchased their homes and started their own families. My oldest brother and his wife, whom now live in Cleveland, Ohio had two girls before I was born; so I had at least one, if not two nieces who were older than me by about one year or so. Talk about a hugh family, well, it was indeed!!

Now, I was born in July, 1955 and at that time I had many older siblings; two of which were born after my birth. Now, why did I go on to mention my small forehead and this cow-lick? Because, I have been teased in school about in the early elementary school years. One thing for sure, when combing my hair; my part was always natural and to this day, the ole cow-lick is still with me . . . and has not disappeared. (scared for life by cowlicks, how funny!!!). I can remember getting up for school, running a comb through my thick brown hair and because of this unfortunate cow-lick that ran across my forehead, I was never able to wear bangs very well. If my hair was cut too short in front, they would stick straight up in front . . . how funny, guess I could have tried using "plaster-of-paris" to get them to lay down. However I do remember Mother using a particular hair product called "Dippity-do". I'm sure some of you remember what I'm talking about . . . . she would dip her hands in the jar of "dippity-do", run them along strands of my hair and then put rollers in; just so I could have curly hair. Sometimes, I would have to wear these rollers to bed and oh I can remember how these things would make my head hurt the next morning; but nothing doing—especially around Easter or Christmas time, she always had to curl our hair. One thing for sure, I was a "girly-girl". So, you see God made me with these small details for me so I could easily be set-apart from everybody else. But, we gotta find humor in some of our "make-up", right? Well, what-ever, let's move along to more important things!!!!

We were a happy family for the most part, each one of us playing a hugh role in duties around the house. We didn't have time to "sit-around" and wonder if mother had anything for us to do; if so, she came looking for us. We were taught the basic principals and values of christian living. Mother always made sure that all of her children were in church on a regular basis and it didn't matter who was born first or who was born last; church was a hugh part of our lives and . . . so, if the church bells were ringing, you can bet ya, we were there within the four walls of our steepled church. Coming from a christian home; my mother was a firm believer in tithing; whether it was little or much; she always gave money in the offering plate as it passed the pews on Sunday mornings. With me being small; I just could not understand why mother would give money to the church like that . . . I just didn't understand it, especially coming from a poor family like we had. We always looked forward to the one week vacation Bible school during the summer while we were out on regular school break; ya know, we had an awesome bunch of fun things to do, like crafts, learn Bible verses, learn new songs and of course, we don't want to forget the wonderful, tasteful cookies and kool-aid they fed us. And, then sometime throughout the year; the church was always holding some type of tent revivals and if they were held outside—the whole community heard good singing and preaching for it's entirety. It was the simple things in life that makes one happy—it's not how much money you had in the bank or how popular a person was in school. We lived a very simple life and that was all there was to it.

My father, being the coal miner that he was, worked very hard for his pay, went to work everyday and never called in sick, that I know of. He was so faithful to show up on time to work and he brought his weekly check home and gave to mother to pay bills and so forth. He toiled and labored miles and miles back inside the mines; working five day week and even on ocassion, he was sometime called in for overtime when someone could not make their shift. He wasn't one of these men who laid around the house and would not work because he knew he had a family to feed. Now when he wasn't back inside the mines digging dark coal out of the ground then his mind was clear of getting his seeds, plants and equipment in order to raise his very large garden every year. I have to stop right here and just imagine my father, tired and exhausted from working this hard; only to come home with much more tasks that followed by being the leader of his home. But, it's certainly not like he didn't have any help plowing the fields and getting them ready for sowing in the spring, oh, I guess that is why he had such a hugh family for!! Help and they helped, indeed.

Seven brothers and seven sisters, plus me. Yes, it was a big family, in fact in today's society, couples today just don't have this many children in their families. I personally know of a few people who come from large families with just as many brothers and sisters. Not too many years ago, the oldest brother living purchased some property in West Virginia right on top of a mountain. He sent word throughout the family that he wanted a name for it and one of the sisters came up with "Mt. Vernon"; so that's what he went with. He decided to have the reunions on top of Mt. Vernon every year, he and his wife was excited to know the family could come home and join one another in love, share memories and come back the next year. Well, this first reunion was about five years ago went well and had a pretty good turn out. Now, it seems the family has grown apart and they are not close anymore. I don't know why. I have tired to figure it out; but it's beyond me and I just cannot wrap my mind around what has happened to this christian family we were all brought up in. I'm probably as safe to say that a lot of it is "jealously of one another". The girls talk about the others and I think the boys have just went their separate ways and just got tired of it all. Cheesy I know, but the truth is my family cannot get along with one another. Just maybe, by a slim chance, some of them reading this book will have a turned heart and come together in love. I would love to see this happen, honestly. This is not the way we were brought up; but each has to answer for what they've done wrong to the others. I love my brothers and sisters very much and I've heard my pastor preach a sermon just the other week, . . . "things may not be the way we want them now; the mess of our lives; but I am going to look to Him to work in my life". I'm going to rely on Jesus. I don't have to have it figured out because God has it figured out for me. We may not see things turn around in our time; but God will fix things on the other side when He returns for His bride.

# Chapter 4

## *Fatigue and Frazzled At Days End*

Have you ever wondered what it's like to have a hugh garden to work up every spring?, well, that what my father had to do and he knew in his heart there would be no worries which would keep him away at night because just knowing he was able to feed his family through the winter months was enough for him. All of the brothers and sisters helped with the gardening and tended it well. I can remember the older ones going out early at day-break and they would hoe the corn; beans and potatoes and any other weeds that may take over the garden and ruin the crops. One of the brothers had worked in the garden planting, hoeing, doing all sorts of things that morning; he spent all day in the field, was extremely hot that day, he was sweaty, dirty and tired. He went to take a break from his labor; saw what he thought was a jug of water and before anyone could stop him; he turned

20

it up and began guzzling down what he thought was water only it turned out to be a gallon jug of gasoline. I don't recall all the events that happened after that . . . but I do remember they took him to the hospital and almost died on the way. Those of us who are mothers now can relate to the fear that came upon my father and mother at that split second of tragedy. But, they reached the hospital in time; pumped his stomach and not certain; but probably kept him overnight for observation and discharged him the following day. My oh my, those days of living with many and many children to keep track of would have been overwhelming for my mother and father, I quite certain of that.

Every year during the summer months, my mother would get the jars with lids ready along with her other canning gear so she could put up the stock for the winter months. Come late October we were very appreciative of the hard work everyone in the family gave in order to sustain life for the winter. Then, it wouldn't be long and I could feel those cold winds beneath my feet and knew it was going to be a long cold winter. Let me say this, in the winter months, it was nothing for those cold winter winds to blow across that mountain top where we lived. I still see those massive amounts of snow drifts; why, it was nothing to see a foot deep of snow fall back then; and everybody knew they had to do their part to gather the crops from the fields before winter. We did not live in royalty as they say . . . we didn't have one of those thermostats in our home where all we had to do was up the degrees by a few and our house was heated . . . . no, we heated our small house on the hill with coal that he dug out of those dark mines at night. I might want to mention also this thermostat did not control any type of central air conditioning for the house. We put these electric fans in the windows, during the day and my goodness all that did was just blew hot air around in the room; but it did keep from getting stuffy in the house and at night it brought the cool air in the house which did allow for better sleeping. Now, I am not quite sure; but I would imagine he didn't get the coal for free—but I'm sure he probably paid a small amount for a truck-load.

My father would bring the coal in by truck load every winter and I can remember him shoveling this massive amount of black coal into the furnace downstairs and firing it up at night to make sure it heated during the night. Mother cooked all meals (breakfast, dinner and supper) on the woodstove. It seemed like all I ever remember her doing was cooking, cleaning and doing the wash every day; from sun up to sun down and when she had finished one meal; it was time to start on another meal. Some of you know what I mean here; especially with that many children to feed in the family. We were always glad to see the spring come because the cold air blew through those thin walls; my goodness, it was like we were camping outside in a tent. Sometimes we all huddled around the wood-stove to keep warm. Talking about the woodstove, I can remember my father coming in from his late night, third shift job in the coalmines, arriving early in the morning. He would sit with his coffee in hand around that old woodstove, nodding his head trying to stay awake. This stove had a round vent that came up from the bottom of the stove; it had a curve in it so far up and this vent lead outside so the fumes from the stove escape in that direction. In between getting cups of coffee—he would sit by the wood-stove and roll his own cigarettes with tobacco that came in the "Prince Albert" can. I often wondered how he kept from burning his fingers with making his own cigarettes; but he did have a "yellowish" tint to his pointer finger from smoking them. He had it down-pat though . . . he would get this small piece of really thin rolling paper; put his tobacco in . . . lick it on one end and seal it shut. Once he got that mastered—he would light that thing up and smoke it along with his coffee in hand. We would also warm our mittens, gloves, hats, and all other by the wood stove too. So, this wood stove that my father kept burning was good for all sorts of things and so thankful to have it; kept us warm, cooked our food on it; warmed our outer wear on it, etc.

Now I can remember only getting a few spankings when I was young; (sure I deserved every one of them) but I don't remember how old I was; but I was old enough to walk. Have you ever had to go outside and cut a switch from one of the bushes or trees? If not, you are lucky because we had to go out and cut our own switches from the branches off the trees. That is not a pretty sight because we knew breaking off that switch was going to be used on our bottom. I started out into the garden one time and stepped on some of the tomato plants that my father had just worked so hard in getting in the ground and I'm telling you, my father was not happy with me. So, I remember very well the spanking I got that evening. I never went back to the garden after that, in fact; I started to head in that direction one summer and heard my father saying "young lady you go back in the house". So in no uncertain terms I knew I must obey! So I did and never went that direction again until I had gotten older and realized how much hard work was involved in planting and seeding the garden with love and care. We were all loved each one by our father and mother, but they also used strick discipline as they handed down rules and regulations that we were to abide by their guidelines. They conducted their authority and corrected us when needed. We knew never to "talk-back" because if we did; we knew what was coming our way and that was not going to be pleasant. Again, we were loved by our father and mother and I can not stress how important it is and even applies in todays society as I have seen discipline from some parents are thrown out the window; and when you don't have it at home, you certainly won't have it in the schools or anywhere else for that matter. We did with what we had and had what we did, times were hard . . . and, we all got along just fine.

Funny, but can you imagine all the children talking at the same time, some fussing, others fighting about what their chores were and how much harder they had to work then others? That did not sit well with our parents because we all knew they needed help whether it be on the inside or the outside—much work was needed.

# Chapter 5

## *General Games, Jacks, Marbles and Much More*

Growing up; we certainly did not have the luxury of many toys to play with; so we would play with old tires that my father had taken off the vehicles because they were worn and no account for anything, we would get those things rolling them down the hills and sometimes one of the siblings would even get inside the tire as it rolling down the hill. Talk about a headache! And I can remember playing marbles with my brothers and sisters at home. I can still see those marbles and how majestic they were so were, so clear with "cat-eyes", well, that's what we called them. Most often, these marbles came in a bag from the local dime store or thrift store and we would make way outside in the dirt to roll these marbles so they would collide into each other when playing with them. We also had a set of jacks and us girls would play that game until our hands got tired, way into the evening hours on the kitchen floor or kitchen table playing this game. Oh the love we shared in the evening on special games like this one. I could never "swish" those jacks up in large handfulls because my hands were too small and I wasn't fast enough to do that and catch the ball at the same time . . . but some of the girls could and probably could go up against anybody in a competition of "playing jacks". They had plenty of practice . . . day in and day out they became to be a pro at this sister's game. I do recall playing "pick-up-sticks"; trying to pick up these colored sticks which were pretty long in nature and we absolutely could not let them touch the other sticks leaning against the others lying on the floor. We also played the childhood game of jump rope. Now, this is one thing I could not do for a while. It took lots of balance and lots of practice to be able to jump in and continue jumping and then another sister would jump in and repeat. Now, these sisters would jump for hours and hours, jumping up and down trying to keep the rope from touching our feet. We played tag outside and hide and go seek which was always a fun game. We had another game we came up with and it was called "roll-over; send-the-ball-over". Now this consisted of throwing a ball over the top of the house and trying to catch it when it rolled over and down the top of the roof. When we were on one side of the house; we would yell out "roll over, roll over, send the ball over". We would stand waiting patiently on the other side of the house waiting for the ball to roll down the other side of the house. When we finally saw the ball coming; we would all try to catch it so we could send the ball back over the house to the ones on the other side. Now, I know that sounds boring and much like a silly game . . . but, we had fun doing all the fun things when I was a little girl. Ya see, we had no video games or such; we just made up things to do to keep ourselves entertained. We also had many other things to do outside for entertainment. We would go into the woods not far from the house and ride down "grape vines". Yes, somehow we made swings out of those grape vines—we would grab ahold of those vines and away we would go swinging back and forth. What good times those were . . . sometimes they would break and down we'd go—just by God's grace we never broke any bones or ended up in the local hospital closeby, so when we fell; we just jumped right back up and headed off to find another vine to swing on. We'd just get up and find more of them and hopefully they wouldn't break on us.

We mastered the nack of climbing up and down trees and walked the split rail fences of the local farmers closeby. Talking about the rail fences; I remember when one of my sisters tore her leg open on a barbed-wire fence and had to have many, many stitches in it. She still has the scar today from that fall. Goodness, we lived dangerously everyday with all the extra energy we had and by evening we would all be exhausted with the many things we would all get into. We didn't have time to be bored, as we hear the children today say they are bored and only been out of school for a week. Many times we went down to the streams and up the hollars and go wading in the water, but we always had to watch out for broken glass and bottles. So many streams up the hollars of West Virginia were dangerous to swim in or wade out into them. But when you're hot from running, hopping, climbing and all sorts of things on these hot summer days, we were thankful to see any type of stream so we could get cooled off for a while. My father would sometimes load all the kids into the back of his pick-up truck and we would head out for a swim in the lake. None of us had bathing suits, so we would just swim with a pair of the boys cut-off jeans and tee-shirts. That made for a fun day at the lake, especially when it was hot and humid in the months of July or August. None of us knew how to swim, so we would just kick around in the water mainly to cool off and have fun. Then, up the streams not too far from the house, we'd catch tadpoles and lighting bugs during the summer and put them in jars. Funny, but I can remember on many times after we'd catch those lighting bugs, taking them home and putting them on a stand in the bedroom and watch them at night after mother would turn the lights out for the night. There was all kinds of things we got into during those hot, sweaty summer nights. Always on the forth of July; we would celebrate at the lake with swimming and picnics. We'd pack up a cooler full of lunch meat, bread, tomatoes and of course we all had to have watermelons. Daddy and Mother would find them a cool shade tree to sit under while we played in the water; they'd set up for a picnic at the park as well.

My memory was very clear on this, we were not allowed to play cards or dance because mother just did not permit us to even think about a deck of cards or going to any school dances. She was very strick, but it was just the mother's love and her protection she had for all of her children. It's not like she was finding ways to keep us from activities at the school house, she was very protective of where we were at all times. We just had certain rules we had to abide by. We were a poor family trying to get by with so little, but we were rich in so many other  ways. We knew we had parents that loved us and did all they could do for so many that they had to buy for. We did not go to the movies and back then they had no such thing as renting movies. Even if they did, we didn't have anything at home to watch them with. We had the old black and white television; but had no DVR's or anything like that to rent movies at home.

# Chapter 6

## *Mother's Meals At Supper Time*

Can one imagine cooking for an army?, Well, that's what it was like when meals were prepared at my house. With much anticipation I can barely wait to tell you you all about mother's mouth watering yeast rolls she used to make and made them pretty often. Her day began early in the morning for a task that took almost a day to making these yeast rolls. She had no recipe, but I do recall mother's items consisted of flour; salt, yeast; canned milk; sugar and plenty of oil. After she got the ingredients together in a pretty large bowl; she would work and work this dough down several times and let them rise, kneading it with her hands, until about the third time of rising; she would pull apart a small amount of dough, making a perfect ball shape, repeating the process until the bowl was empty. Then she would put them in to bake and you could smell the aroma all over the house while they were baking. After she took these rolls out of the oven, oh my, they were so pretty and brown when done. No kidding at all, these rolls literally was like eating pastries and just the best yeast rolls in town and for that matter, in the world or so I thought. One can only wish for certain things sometimes and if I were wishing for something right now; it would be to have just one more batch of these, oh so delightful yeast rolls to put on my table for dinner and absolutely no-one could make them like she could. She made them so often, she always knew exactly how much to put of this and that to get them to taste just right. This seems so simple to be talking about meals and so forth; but since I'm on the subject, I just might as well tell you about some of mother and daddy's down home "cooking" and "farming" they used to do.

Now, generally it was a "given" that mother would always return thanks for our meal and it was considered "family time" at the supper table. We did not share events of the day; we were just trying to get our stomachs full before the bowls went empty on the table because some siblings around the table didn't know what the word "share" meant. Mother always made large portions of everything, she always served hot bread of some sorts, whether it was biscuits; cornbread or just plain loaf of hot white bread. She cooked large amounts of potatoes and green beans and that was surely to fill anyone's stomach full.

Mother put away many, and I say many jars of green beans, corn, pickles and other fresh vegetables from the hugh garden my father toiled in every year. I can remember sitting on the back porch of the house snapping green beans. Now, keep in mind I was just little, but it did not matter how little you were, if there was work to be done, we were taught how to do it and snapping green beans on that back porch was the thing mother taught me that particular day. That was probably one of my most least favorite jobs around the house; but we had to do it. We not only had to pick the beans; but had to help snap them as well. Don't want to fuss too much though because I sure did enjoy the meals that came from the hard work of helping to can them. I remember she had the water boiling on the woodstove and would put those jars of beans, corn or tomatoes down in that hot water. I fully didn't understand the concepts of cooking and canning, but as I got older it seemed to make more sense to me. Mother would put her apron on and stand on her feet all day long getting that produce into jars and onto the shelves for winter. Boy, that was good stuff and I'm not kidding one bit!!

With the fruits we gathered from peach trees, strawberry plants and we'd pick apples from the apple trees in the fall, and soon mother was canning many jams and jellies. It was a real treat for her to make a peach cobbler or blackberry cobbler for a dinner meal. In the early spring, we would all pile in the back of the pick up truck with our strawberry buckets in hand and pick those berries for jams and jellies. Then, in the latter months of summer, we would gather our pales and head out to pick blackberries on the sides of the road . . . most of them country roads in the state of West Virginia. I remember my father would most always reminds us to "watch out for snakes around those berry vines". That used to scare me to think there maybe snakes closeby—but God always took care of us. We spent most of our summers doing chores around the house and helping mother put up the fruits of our labor. We would leave on early Saturday mornings and not come back until our pales were full. We ate on this all winter long until the next year would roll around only to do it all over again. Oh, the memories of home!! I'm quite sure there are plenty of people that can relate to my same similar situations that we called home in the hills of West Virginia. But ya know, we all got along just fine.

My father and mother were well known in the neighborhood and liked by everyone. When they weren't doing for their own family; they were doing for others, putting others first and thinking of their needs. I can remember mother telling me she had to feed the "hobos" that were riding the train coming into town. Why in the world was she feeding them, I thought to myself? She never wanted anybody to go hungry and since the railroad tracks ran right behind our house; the hobos would get off and mother would feed them. They were never allow to come in the house and had to stay outside; but she fed them well. But, you know; they kept busy day by night with many tasks at hand, things to keep them occupied around the house. My father at that time in his life worked mostly at night while we were in bed sleeping. He came home in the early morning hours while we were at school. I can remember when he came in from the mines, his face would be black as coal dirt and we young'uns would rush to get his lunch pale (which was a silver bucket that was a two-tier) to see if he left us any snack or cake that he might not have eaten and saved it for us.

Again, let me remind you; the oldest ones were married and left home before I was born. I don't remember so much about the older siblings but only a few things; I was just too young. We were poor, but, all of us were happy because we did not know of anything else but happiness. God took care of us, some how, some way and we all got along just fine! We were a very poor family but rich in spirit. What would I mean by that? Mother made sure we were in church because going to church was a big part of our lives. She kept her Bible close by at all times, constantly reading it and studying it. I can remember passing by her bedroom door one day when I was small, took a "peek-in" to see what she was doing because I heard her talking to someone. I thought to myself; what is she doing in there? So, upon my surprise, she was kneeling down by the bed; on her knees praying to God. She was crying out to him that one particular morning and just wish I could remember what she was saying. I do remember that made a hugh impact on my life and how much faith she had. She not only talked the talk; she walked it; loved it; knew it and prayed for it. My father would not go to church with us as a family, why?, I don't know but he always stayed home. She made sure every morning before we left for school that we read the Bible before we left of a morning. She always would say, "kids, come on—it's time to read the Bible" before you leave. After she read the Bible to us, we would have prayer and then it was off to that long dreaded walk or run to that ole school house that seemed so far away. But, God got us through the rough days of living on the hill in Leivasy, West Virginia. We were happy and just got along just fine. I remember turning into my pre-teens; maybe a little older when "Dolly Pardon" came out with a song titled "The Coat Of Many Colors, My Mother Made For Me". All I could think about was that song and how mother sewed and the many quilts she made for the beds. The fabric she used to make the quilts were from the cloth she purchased to make our dresses or the boys clothes and so that song reminded me of these quilts, you see. It's still freshly etched in my mind these many quilts she would sew by hand and my how did they come in handy at night to keep us warm on the cold winter nights.

# Chapter 7

## *Stringing Berries and Popcorn Every Year For The Tree*

Now, I am going to share with you some of what our Christmas mornings and memories at home were like. I can recall times were difficult for my father because, I'm sure in his mind; he probably felt this extremely amount of pressure on his shoulders to try and figure out how to get some gifts wrapped and under the tree for his children come Christmas morning. He barely made enough money to pay the bills; much less have to purchase Christmas gifts for all of us . . . well, at that time there were 7 or 8 of us still living at home and can you imagine buying presents for that many children?. Well, my parents did what they could and what they could afford. Oh yes, sitting on the couch in the late evenings with my sisters turning the pages in the Sears Roebuck Toy Wish Book looking at the toys and the dolls in that book every year. It was as if Christmas had already arrived in our home; true, not a single family member knew what I was thinking in my mind as I turned the pages over and over, wishing I could have some of those baby dolls in that Sears Roebuck Toys Wish Book; but to no avail, none of us would benefit from spending hours looking at those toys on the pages. We considered it a real treat just to sit down side by side and look through the book and only "wish". My goodness, I would spend hours looking at the toys in that book and think to myself; if only I would be surprised on this particular Christmas morning. Now this book entertained us for hours, it seemed; but our real joy for Christmas was knowing we would get to decorate the tree. Folks, that was memories and memories I never want to forget. We were poor; but we all got along just fine.

So, now comes the best time of the year as my father has cut the tree down and bringing it home so we could decorate it Christmas eve. It seems to always be a snow storm that blew across that mountain top during that special holiday but he managed to get the tree cut down, drag it home; and ya know that's when our excitement began. We popped popcorn . . . . not the microwave kind, but the kind of corn you put in the iron skillet and pushed it back and forth across the wood stove until it started popping. My goodness, I can remember the days of excitement when we would start getting the tree prepared and adorned with lights and how thrilling it was to get this tree exactly the way we wanted it to look. So, we would string that popcorn by way of threading it piece by piece on this tread that mother gave us out of her sewing basket; we also would string red berries from the holly bush around the tree. We made any type of homemade ornaments with crayons and white paper and hung them on the tree. I really don't remember if any of us kids had a stocking; but I'm sure we had one because I do remember getting fruit in these old white socks. In those socks we would get a couple pieces of fruit; an apple, an orange and plenty of nuts. We used to get pretty excited about that . . . all of us would dance and prance around the living room. You would have thought we got a million dollars in those old white socks! We were very thankful because we knew that was all my father and mother could afford.

Also, for some very practical gifts, mother would purchase fabric from the local merchants and she would make dresses for the girls for Christmas; well, one or two a piece. She would make the boys their shirts and pants; carefully wrapping them up in newspapers and laying them under the tree. Some of the older brothers and sisters whom had already gotten married and left home to start their own homes; would surprise us and buy a box of crayons and coloring book for all of us to put under the tree for Christmas. Sometimes they would get us a paddle-ball set and we enjoyed those. But that was all folks we got for Christmas and we did not know any better than to be unappreciative for what we got. We were so excited to get what we got. I do remember one Christmas my father and mother bought me a doll and her name was "Skipper". I don't think I got any extra clothes for it—just what came on the doll when they purchased it. I was so excited about that doll. There's a picture recently given to me from a few months back of my twin brother and sister who was on a tricycle and my sister had a doll baby in her hands. That was such a cute picture of them. So, our special Christmas was bleek every year but truly a blessed one and we were one happy bunch of kids to have gotten very little. Other memorable things that mother would do on a regular basis was that she made every piece of clothing we wore. I remember she couldn't afford to buy patterns at the local market; so she would cut patterns out by newspapers. As I mentioned above about the fabric she bought at the local markets . . . she really did make every Easter dresses all the girls wore and made the boys their shirts and pants. We were always so proud to for a special holiday to come around because we all knew we were getting new dresses. Before the school year began, she would start early so she could get out clothes sewed up in time for school. My father and mother couldn't afford shoes for us; so we just wore what ever we could find. Times were hard—but we had food to eat and we had each other. I rarely remember the worse of the worse hard times up on the hill of Leivasy; but I do remember some things that I would not want to take back for nothing. The best part of living on the hillside in Leivasy, West Virginia was our mother taking the time to read the Bible to us before we left for the school house each morning. We had a dog named Lassy (German Shepherd) and when mother began to pray for our safety to and from school; that dog would bark along with the prayers that mother lifted up before God. I remember so well Lassy always knew when to come onto the front porch, then he would walk us to school.

# Chapter 8

## *Skipping Off To The Ole School-Yard!*

It seems like miles and miles, and so far to go. Being kids; sometimes we all do things some what different and I remember coming home from school one afternoon in the early month of May; some of us had taken a different route back home and went by way of "Lanham's Swinging Bridge". This bridge was at the back of the house and the house was right along side the road. We were always told to not walk on or near the highway. But the story doesn't stop here . . . now this old swinging bridge did not look safe to cross or anything . . . but being a little precarious, we willing to try anything out for the first time. So looking from one end to the other, this swinging bridge would go up and down, up and down, swaying back and forth. Scary to think anyone would cross that thing . . . . but this brave little girl started out across it and it began to swing causing the underboards to buckle from the weight of the movements. It was too late for me to turn around and go back so I proceeded on across the bridge. One of my brothers was at the end of the swinging bridge; jumping up and down on it and to make matters worse for me; he began jumping on the end of it and I fell off that bridge into the water below. Now, thank goodness the water was not deep, it was more like a small stream; but still the bridge had height to it and it was a long way into the water from having fallen in. I remember standing up and my clothes were wet I did not get hurt any; but all I could think about was what my mother was going to say when I got home. I mean, you can not hide wet clothes. Now the owners of that bridge, Lanham's were either not home or just did not care that I had fallen because they did not come out to see if I was hurt or not. I got on dry land and walked home with my clothes wet and I remember mother gave me an old fashion spanking for taking a different route home from school and not coming in a group. My brother that shook the bridge got a whipping too for making me fall. Now, there were some of the brothers that was more inquistive than others. What I mean by that is this? We were always looking for things to do differently or get into some kind of trouble. There was one particular brother who liked to take things apart (like the iron, mixer and any thing that was electric) to figure out how the thing works and would put it back together again. Mother would go to make a cake and the cord would be cut off from her mixer. Now there was no humor in these sorts of things and mother had very little patience when it come to this kind of stuff. It was things like this that mother felt like whipping them good. Oh, and did I mention school? Yes, we did not ride the school bus to the grade school. We walked or ran to make sure we were there before the bell rang. It was a small grade school there in Leivasy. Just a small school and I think at that time the school went to the 5th or 6th grade. Each of my siblings were there in each grade of the school. Well, that is the ones left at home when I was born. It's funny to look back on that now, we laugh, we cry, but we got along just fine.

I remember we were never allow to eat in the school cafeteria because the expense was way much more than our parent's weekly budget. We seldom packed a lunch from home because honestly, we never had anything to pack in a brown lunch bag. We would run home from school for lunch and then run back to make sure we didn't miss the bell from ringing tardy. Now, I am not sure how many miles or even city blocks it was but if we were to measure it today—I'm sure it would be well over two miles from school to home. I remember sometimes arriving at home for lunch only to get a "fried biscuit" and then running all the way back. I can remember how tired my little legs were when I got back to that classroom. Exhausted from the trip, all I wanted to do in that class room was catch my breath and listen at the teacher all at the same time.

I can remember on good days at the ole school house, (you know, all teachers have their favorites) and they would choose different students to go out in the afternoon to dust her chalk board erasers on this big old wooden stump out beside the school. Someone had cut the tree down and left the stump, so on our good behavior . . . Now, I remember the teacher picking her favorites out of the classroom to dust her erasers, and I can remember one time she picked me. I thought to myself, why would she pick me? But, for some reason I felt this gave me some sense of "somebody" to get to dust the erasers for the teachers. How funny; but back then that was a big deal. I have since learned that they tore down that ole school house and re-built a new one. It's still called Leivasy Grade School. Not too long ago some of us sisters went back up there on the hill to call back the memories and past events in our mind; and while there, before we headed back off the hill; we decided to take a picture of us standing beside that new school house on the hill in Leivasy, West Virginia.

I can remember we were even allowed to wear pants to school because mother thought girls should dress like girls and boys should dress like boys. We were poor; but we all got along just fine! Yet, on many, many ocassions we headed off to that ole school house on the hill in Leivasy with the soles of our shoes flapping because my father and mother just could not afford to purchase school clothes and shoes for all their children to wear. I can remember sliding my foot along and all down the halls of that ole school house on the hill and it was really embarrasing to try and walk proudly in front of the other school mates who went to school there. Why, my goodness, those shoes were not fit to wear outside to play in; much less to wear to that old school house on the hill. There were plenty of children in the neighborhood and around that were just as poor as we were. Some did not have much and then others were better off than others going to school and we got along just fine. So, now I am moving into my middle school years . . . not quite sure how old I was when my father applied for a mining job in the state of Ohio. It seemed I always carried such a low self esteem of myself. Probably because I never received any encouragement from family.

# Chapter 9

## *Crossing Over The Ohio River Bridge*

All I can remember at that time was my parents telling us we were going to move to Ohio. I thought to myself; I wonder if we'll have a bigger house and all kind of thoughts running through my mind about moving away from our Leivasy homeplace. We had to pack up our stuff (which wasn't much) and move, move away from our homeplace. I just didn't like changes for that matter and could not wrap my mind around moving away. So, moving day came and all I can remember is loading up our belongings, which were few—and heading up the road, crossing the Ohio River Bridge heading toward a little town called Dennison, Ohio. Now, I am sure everyone has seen the series on television "The Beverly Hillbillies"—well, I'm just quite certain we looked like the folks on that show, except we weren't moving to California where black gold was struck. I remember my father and mother had rented a house from this farmer out in the middle of no-where . . . of which we all called "The Stocker's Home" located in Dennison, Ohio. Now, this house was hugh—plenty of rooms. I remember this old house had a barn not too far from the house. All of us kids liked going into that old barn . . . setting out to be inquistive of what possibly could be in there we could play with. This was all brand new stuff to us . . . never being around anything like this before—we knew there must be something, like old things, things we could do; jump in hay and all sorts of stuff. I remember seeing lots of hay, I remember chicken and cows. And, I remember when we were caught playing up in the barn and the owner "Mr. Stocker" hollared out to us kids . . . "ya'll had better stay out of that barn and I don't want you playing in there". Well, I just thought he was the meanest person around to not let us play in the attic of that barn—I mean after all, what was so important in there that we could not play; knew we could not hurt anything. Off we went to school and when the bus dropped us off; guess what . . . we headed back into the barn that afternoon after school. We had made several trips over to the barn to play when all of a sudden we looked over leaning up beside the dark wooden boards of that barn was a bicycle that was truly coated in dust of probably an inch thick. Well, you would have thought we found a million dollars . . . if looking in the mirror; our eyes were probably as big as saucers. We did, we had found an old bicycle to ride  and I think we all learned how to ride that bike in that old barn. We could hardly wait to get on that thing so we all took turns riding that bicycle up in that barn and the dust was flying from all the hay up there. We had the time of our life riding that thing. Then, we heard our mother calling us to come home for dinner.

We rushed home; washed up because you definitely did not come to mother's dinner table with dirty hands or face. Could you not see it now . . . all of us around a wash pot trying to get clean hands and face so we could sit down at the dinner table? It seems we engulfed our food in whole pieces and could hardly wait to get back to the barn to ride that old rattle trap of a bicycle again. Why, that thing was so rusty and didn't even have air in the tires . . . but we didn't care. I do remember it had rusted fenders on it, front and back. So, at my small age (I don't remember how old I was, maybe 9 or 10 years old) I learned to ride that bicycle in that attic barn. It was hard for me to sleep at night because of the excitement of that bike because you see, with money so tight in our family we never had a bicycle to call our own. This is funny but true—my brother Martin would take that bicycle out on the road that ran in front of that old big white house—get to going really fast and slam on the brakes and the sparks would just fly because he took the tires off it (well, they were flat anyway) and we certainly didn't have any way of putting air in that old thing.

I can not remember if we had a garden there or not. I'm quite sure we did—but just don't remember it. That old house "The Stockers" was big and white. We had a sidewalk that went down from the front steps to the main little farm road that ran in front of the house. I remember mother had undoubtedly spoke to someone local and was able to get the milk man to deliver milk to the front steps of the house. I remember the milk-man coming by early and drop off bottles of milk. Rarely would mother get us chocolate milk—but sometimes she would. It was such a treat for us to sit down at the table and drink chocolate milk with our homemade biscuits. Those memories are etched in my mind forever. One thing I also remember about "The Stocker's House" was mother always thought it was haunted. Now, for me being as little as I was I was frightened about that. She would sit down at the dinner table and tell us stories or if you call them "tales" of "hearing chains rattling" upstairs in that one particular bedroom. I was so scared of that house I could barely find myself going upstairs to bed at night. Some of my older siblings had gotten married and they came to visit us there at "The Stockers" in Dennison., Ohio. I remember they would sit downstairs in the living area telling "ghost stories" at night. I'm sure it was because mother always said the house was haunted and the things she heard just prompted the ghost stories. Over all, those were pretty good times living there in that big old white house called "The Stockers". We left that place because my father wanted to buy a house in Tippecanoe, Ohio. He was still working for the same coal mining company, just moving to purchase a house.

So, off we moved again to a house that my father and mother had purchased for probably hardly no money involved. Why, this house didn't even have a bathroom in it. But that wasn't anything new (none of the houses we lived in so far had indoor bathrooms in them) So, I remember when my father put one in—he built it himself. It was small, but we did have a tub, commode and sink in it. We had met most of the neighbors in that small little town and got acquainted with them. We made friends and found us getting along with everyone. There we would remain for a few years while my father toiled and worked in the coal mines deep down in the earth in that state of Ohio. Funny, but true—we enrolled in the school house there in Freeport, Ohio. Mother found out from the school board that we would be riding the school bus to and from me . . . yipee, no more running and walking to school. So, time for school to start in September and we'd get to ride on a big orange bus. I guess every state had their own colors of school buses and I do remember our school buses there in that great state of Ohio being orange. I think I was about 11 or 12 years old at that time. While we were at school, mother was out trying to find us a local church where we could all attend. After searching for about a week or so; she found one and again it was a Nazarene Church. She would always make us sit on the front row and she would sit behind us to make sure we behaved in church. If we didn't, we knew what was coming when we got home. On rare ocassions, one of us had to get up and go sit with her because we were acting up in church. My father would not go to church with us, for you see he never wanted any part of it—I don't know why; but I guess he had his reasons for not going. But he never stopped our mother going and taking us. I loved my father and I respected him because he did what he had to to keep the family going from year to year. He placed a roof over my head and put food on the table, so how could anyone not be thankful for those things?

Now, we did not have a dryer in the house. We had a ringer type washing machine and this washing machine sat out on the back porch of our house. I remember she had this hugh metal barrel and she had it sitting on top of another table; lower than the ringer on the washing machine. Inside this barrel contained a starch and water mixture and after the clothes washed in that ole washing machine, she would guide the clothes through that ringer into that barrel of water and starch. She would hand rinse the clothes (whether they were sheets or towels) or just maybe our trousers or dresses up and down into that water and guide them back into that ringer washing machine. After she got them rinsed well, she would put them into a basket and off to the clothes line we would go, baskets in hand. This typically was an all day Saturday job and we would have to hang up the clothes up on the line to dry. I remember my father made these wooden poles that would go under the lines and after we got the clothes hung up; mother would take those poles and stand them straight up in the air to keep the clothes from dragging down the line and getting the clothes dirty from the ground. The clothes would dry and then it was a repeat after that—until the laundry was done. I can remember mother putting water into a bowl; then she would reach her hands into this water and sprinkle them over these dried clothes and then roll them up. I thought to myself, "she hung them on the line to dry and now she is sprinking water on them"? I was old enough to understand the process and did not realize what she was going to do with those clothes that she had sprinkled water on. Little did I know, the older girls would have to iron those baskets of clothes. Now, whether they were sheets, pillow cases, shirts, dresses—all had to be ironed. I don't think I ever had to do any ironing—if I did, I don't remember it. But, I do remember the older sisters would have to iron everything in the basket and put them on hangers, what didn't go on hangers, they folded them neatly in a stack. Oh the memories of home, I could go on and on with them. Times were hard, but we made it through the good and the bad times.

One cold winter Sunday morning we were getting ready for church and the snow was just peppering down outside the house. But that did not stop us from heading to the church. We all piled into the car and headed across the valley heading towards Tappan Lake and I can remember crossing the road that lead to the dam. Well, it was so cold out and still the snow was coming down in bucket fulls and I can remember our car got hung-up in the snow there at the dam of this lake. Well, mother began to pray that God would send someone to help us get our car out of the deep snow. So, after about 30 minutes had passed, mother sent one of the brothers out walking to the end of the road to get help and by the time he got back to the car he was nearly froze. He ended up not finding anyone at the end of the road to help us. There wasn't much traffic on the roads that morning and especially with the snow storm we were having that day. By the time he got back to the car; his toes and hands were frost-bit and I remember he came very near to losing them. So mother prayed feverishly for help to arrive. Not too long after that . . . we all saw how God answered our mothers prayers and God sent this man on a big tractor with a plow and he plowed the road so we could get the car going again. I remember when we got the the car out; we headed back home and did not try to go onto church that morning. Mother loved God and she was a prayer warrior and stepped out on faith so many times and looking back over the years I see how God worked in her life. She never wavered in her faith.

# Chapter 10

## *Terrible Tragedy; The Train Hits The Car*

Now, we have lived in this little town called Tippecanoe for about two years now. We had all gotten acquainted with everyone in the neighborhood and life in Tippecanoe was going along good. We had found a good church, going regularly; liked our little house there and even had indoor plumbing in it. Talk about moving "uptown"—well, we were living life on easy street because of our indoor fixtures with running water and bath room facilities that my father had installed after we moved in the house.

It was a Wednesday afternoon—we had all came in from school, dinner was cooked and we all had ate. My father was in bed sleeping because he had to work the next day. He had moved from night shift into a day shift position not long after we moved to Tippecanoe. It was the fall of the year, September, and the leaves were just beginning to turn and fall from the trees. Most all of the kids and me were going on a hay ride with the church group that Wednesday night. Mother said we could go but she was going on to church. She did not drive and didn't have a drivers license so she depended on my father or older brothers or sisters to get her around town. I can vagely remember this . . . . we were on our way for the hayride when the neighbor came out and told us that we could not go. "What do you mean"?, our mother said we could go. Now, this neighbor lady was nice and all; but I was starting to get mad at her for not letting us go on the hayride with the church group. So we went back together to the house. When we got there, I remember my father leaning over the front porch just weeping. I said to myself—what is going on? Then, I was told that my mother had been killed in a train accident. That was the saddest day of my life. (period) I can remember thinking to myself . . . how could this be?—is it a dream? How can I live my life without my mother? How can I go on? How can we lose our mother? All kinds of questions were running through my mind. At that moment in my life; I felt an emptyness that I have never felt in my life before. I can remember feeling so sad and that sadness was overtaking my every being. Now, I knew of this God that mother had always read and prayed about in the Bible. If God was real; why would He take my mother away and how could my mother be dead from a tragic train accident? I just remember how my father stood over that bannister of that house there on the hill in Tippecanoe just crying like a baby. It just broke the family down and it seemed that none of us could go on living without her. Now the sister who was living at home during the time our mother was killed in this train accident was the oldest and she was the only one who had her drivers license and was able to drive mother to church that night. She was injured in the accident as well. In fact; she had so many injuries she was admitted to the hospital and was unable to attend the funeral of our mother. Did anyone ever think to themself, if only we only had one day and could bring someone back from Heaven; what would that day be like?, how many questions would we have for them, awww questions like . . . . what's it like living in Heaven?, what is can I get for you today?, would you let me take you shopping today, I want to buy you something especially for you!! Those things have crossed my mind many times and I guess just because I'm human and when you miss someone that much and know well within your being they will never return to this earth until God calls him bride home to Heaven with him. But in reality, I would not want to wish anybody that gone on before me back to this sinful earth with so much distruction around us.

Such a tragic time in our life; with so many of us kids still at home, without our mother; but we would just have to figure out how to manage and go on. So many different things happening all at once, where in the world does a person start with life and trying to make some sense of what had happened? I was old enough to know that my mother had been killed in a train accident and my sister was also involved. Now, I heard the sirens going by the house, one that carried my mother and the other one that carried my sister. Even now at my age, when I hear sirens from medics, I get this shiver down my back because I still remember the sounds of those ambulances roaring down the road. I still recall one of the ambulances going really fast pass the house that late September evening and I looked so hard at it to see if I could see mother in the back. Even thought at one point, maybe I could see her moving in it. (just wishful thinking) Well, time went slow for a few days because the older sisters and brothers had to be notified of her death. Most of the older ones were living out of state, so they had to make their way back to Ohio for the funeral. Oh I can remember how sad that was to see this hugh family of ours all together again under one tiny roof. God has His ways of bringing people together and it seemed to satisfy my soul knowing there were older siblings there that I could lean on. Don't know why I felt the way I did, but being young, you just kind of look to older people for some sense of direction.

It was getting late on Thursday evening back in September of 1969 and Friday was the next day. I was going to have to force myself to go to this emotional funeral of my mother. I can remember walking into that Wallace and Wallace Funeral Home in Rainelle, West Virginia and as I came around the corner, looked up to the front of the room, there I saw many, many, many flowers and this casket right in the middle of them. It was so emotional for me and I began to cry. Thoughts went running through my mind like . . . . oh could this be a dream?, am I really dreaming all of this? I tried to compose myself because I knew I had to go up front and see for myself if this was really real. I remember like yesterday starring at her thinking that I actually saw her breathing at one time, but it was just my imagination because I just did not want to accept the fact that my mother had been killed in a train accident. So, we managed to get through the viewing of the body and then the next day it was off to the burial site where they were going to bury my mother. I remember leaving that funeral home so sad and depressed. I felt as though my world came crashing in on top of me and those of you whom have lost your parents at this early young age know exactly what I'm talking about.

Now, from Rainelle, West Virginia to Clintonville to the grave plot where they were going to bury my mother was many miles. I can remember driving and driving—thinking to myself, "how far is this place away?". I was young and didn't realize much about time or distance. We finally arrived after about 30 minutes and around this grave yard we went, up the hills and down until the family car came to a stop. These men (pallbearers) walked to the back of this hugh black car, lifted my mother out of the back of that black car and carried her over underneath this green tent where the gravemen's had dug a hugh hole in the ground. On top of that hole was this vault that they would lower into the ground and that would be the final resting place for my mother until Jesus returns. Her body was in the ground; but her soul went to heaven; but somehow leaving that grave yard, I kept looking back and looking back . . . . leaving there without my mother. I cried and cried for days. I didn't want to go back to school and school was beginning to start. So now I was starting to go into the 8th grade at school. Now, I felt such an emptyness at home even though we had each other. How do people make it through life without a brother or sister? Our father was still living and soon found himself being "father and mother" to all of us left behind when mother was killed so tragically. It was such a sad time in my life and I really did not want to go on living. All I could think about was going to live where my mother was . . . in heaven. Why would I say heaven?, because she was a godly woman with much love for Jesus. I was now beginning to think about her and how much she really loved church and to be in church.

I never had many one on one talks with my mothers and so I never had the opportunity to ask her when she accepted Christ as her personal Savior; and when she repeated the sinner's prayer, I just knew she must have been saved. You've heard the simple song . . . 'you know you are a christian by your love' . . . well, not only that but because of the life she lived for Christ and the active years she spent in church, the faith she lived out. Remember, I shared with you earlier, when she was not in church, she was daily singing around the house. I remember one of her favorite songs were "I come to the arden alone, while the dew is still on the roses" and the voice I hear, falling on my ears, within my heart is singing . . . and He walks with me and He talks with me and He tells me

I am His own". Oh, another one of her favorite songs was "The Ninety and Nine" and she sang that quite often too. Such beautiful spiritual songs she sang . . . such a powerful voice that God gave her, so ya see, she's singing in Heaven's choir now—rejoicing with the angels and everybody that's gone on before her.

Being young we all wanted to feel important and precious to our parents . . . close enough; but now, . . . . I really felt like at that point in my life of drowning myself in my own sorrows and did not want to live without her. Oh yeah, my father was still living; but there is something about "mothers" as read in the book of Proverbs and how much wisdom they have and we all learn from our parents.

# Chapter 11

## *I Must Grow Up Without Mother*

So, my life will continue on without her and we take it one day at a time. Who is going to love me now that my mother is gone? I am now at the inner core of my every being with decisions I had to make, right or wrong, about leaving home; but it was only for three months and felt I could do three months with them back home. But wait; did I say, leaving home?, maybe hidden deep within my heart I wanted to stay close to my father, brothers and sisters. So, the day came that my oldest sister came to visit us living there in Tippecanoe. She and her husband wanted me to come live the summer months with them because they saw my need for some type of "motherly love". They invited me to come down to their home, big plans, hugh plans, they were going to teach me how to water ski and spend the summer with them with much more things to offer than staying home where my life for three months would be boring, needless to say. How could a young girl at a young age of fourteen years pass up the chance? My father agreed with that . . . . so off I came to Charlotte North Carolina. Away from my other brothers and sisters, I came to spend the entire summer. I did learn to water ski and met lots of new friends. That was probably one of the best summers I had or at least that's what I thought at the time. I learned back home that two of my brothers had joined the arm services and one went to Germany; but not quite sure where the other one went. My sister next to me in age went to Charleston to live with one of my eldest sisters who at the time had just recently went through a divorce with her husband and she had two children to raise by herself. So, sis went to live with her; helped her with child-care while the older one worked. By this time, all that's left at home is my father (whom had remarried) and my youngest brother. The rest of us were gone and I guess that was the escape for us trying to find happiness in all the wrong places since our mother had passed away. Sometimes our sorrows in life will either beat us to death or make the best out of us and for that very reason, I was determined to stay positive about everything. I stay for three months in Charlotte, North Carolina. My oldest sister and her husband drove back and forth to Lake Norman where they had their lake lot with a pier. They had a boat and many other fun things to do during the summer months that school was out. On weekends we went to the lake and that's where I learned to water ski. Now, during the week—while in living in Charlotte, I met this young boy whom I felt I could really like. It's funny how young boys will take a liking to young girls. Well, that lasted for just the summer months and the cuteness of this young lad faded away. It was time for me to go back to my father's house; but my sister and her husband decided to enroll me in school down here. My father agreed and so I decided to stay here with them. Why?, I can never answer that question other than; was I scare; was I needed?, was I irresistible? No one wants to be alone or felt alone and I truly didn't want to leave the friends that I had met. Short of a small miracle, I enrolled in school and was literally scare to death of entering my high school days. I don't know why—probably because I wasn't living with my real parents. How was I going to explain all of this to my friends I went to school with? Some of my associates at school thought my sister and her husband were my parents . . . I mean after all, they were old enough to be my parents. I just never went into explaining all of it; but to just a few friends. So, what would I have changed in my life and what could I have done over or lived over in my life at such a young age? I would have remained at home with my father whom I know loved me; being close to my older brothers and sisters for just the security of knowing my life would not have been in harms way of any danger or the hoops I had to jump through for a family member that cared nothing about me or my life. I have been hurt in many ways and knew in my heart things would be better if I had gone back home to my fathers. I should have heeded my heart's desire and acted accordingly.

Living in that environment was hard for me. I'm not going to speak much about it other than I longed for safety and security of my father. I once read a book by the author, Sharon Jaynes and found this book very helpful for me and all the tragic things that happened in my life. This author says it best . . . "at this early point in my life, I was only trying to find a place and purpose of the hurts of my past". I felt by moving away was probably the best for me; but you know what they say . . ." hinesight is better than foresight. God knew I had been hurt and this left with emotional scars on my life. None of us ever want bad things to come in and out of our lives; but I certainly had much to deal with at such a very young age.

All I could think to myself was there must be some type of hope out there for me . . . but I just could not bare the thoughts of talking with anyone. I knew that bringing shame upon a person's life would cause me to not be true to myself. I knew "Of" this God that my mother spoke of when I was growing up at home; but really didn't know Him. I knew that I was wonderfully made in the image of Him and that one day I wanted to know this Jesus. I do know that God was able to take any of my difficult situations and I could learn from them. So, I started praying for His wisdom and guidance in my life—but was not sure God was even hearing my prayers. Only at that point in my life I realized to myself life was hard for me; but somehow in my every being, I was going to have to make some sense of it. I cried a lot; and I cried alot of times. For being a young woman—there was absolutely no happiness in my life what-so-ever. I really wanted to die; but Jesus had other plans for me. I just could not figure out what they were, but I knew someday He would reveal His plan in my life. I lived day by day in a house where Jesus was not talked about much, but my sister and her husband did attend a local church. Looking back now, living in that house meant nothing to me then and and it means nothing to me now.

Those years of my life I would like to erase from my memory and never think about them again. So, here I am; my mother was passed away and my father was living in West Virginia. I remember specifically telling my brother-in-law that I wanted to go home. They drove me home . . . but when we arrived there, things had changed. I should have fell on my knees right then and prayed for God to direct my paths; but satan won over again and I found myself coming back to North Carolina to live with them again. I can remember starting to smoke cigarettes because I felt such a void in my life. I remember coming back from West Virginia one time and on the stretch of I-77 I had told my sister and her husband that I had started smoking and my brother in law stopped the car and told me to get out of the car. He was not going to have me smoking; but it was like I had some type of control by smoking those cigarettes and beginning to get some type of control even though I was not of age to go out on my own. While enrolled in high school; I remember walking into the principals office and telling the principal that I wanted to learn how to drive a school bus. I was in the 10th grade and yes, I started driving that big yellow bus . . . up and down the highways and thoroughfares picking up students and taking them to school. I received a small check every month for driving that thing. I made very little profit; but it was enough for me to buy clothes at this little small downtown shop in Lincolnton, North Carolina that carried a brand-name of "Hang Ten". Now, coming from a very poor family to making money for the very first time was big for me. Money in my pocket and enough to buy me more cigarettes to boot, now I really thought I was living. The day came when my brother-in-law said he was going to have to have me pay for the large tire tracks my bus was leaving behind on the drive down to the house. I can remember giving him my money two or three times that I got paid so he could haul some gravel into those places to cover up the ruts the wheels left behind. I can remember how mad that made me to have to give up my money to him. I was beginning to think this was not fair. I soon had enough money to get my cap and gown, I ordered my invitations to send out to my family that I was graduating from high school and I was getting excited about that. I did all the girly stuff that girls do in high school—I went to the junior prom; went to the senior prom—so forth and so on. I can remember signing up for the senior play and got a part in it but overall I was a very average student in school. I had very poor study habits; but I managed to get my diploma and graduate from high school.

College was of no interest to me—probably because I had no one encouraging me to pursue any other avenues. I did, however; enlist to a small community college in Charlotte, North Carolina and was taking general courses to try and better myself. I quit after a few days because I had found out there had been a kidnapping in the parking deck on the school campus and later found out on the local news that evening, the girl that was kidnapped had been murdered. Now, being eighteen years old and hearing this kind of stuff was too scary for me; out in this great big world with no sense of direction in my life. I have no idea what; if any, type of classes I wanted to take and definitely did not have a clue . . . "what do I want to be when I grow up". So, from then on I was too scare to walk from that parking deck in the daytime; much less the night time classes. So, I quit that school and never went back. Now, you are probably thinking to yourself; doesn't take much to change this girl's mind about anything. Maybe it was the fact that I was searching for some security and stability in my life . . . something that I had never had especially since my mother had passed away.

# Chapter 12

## *Preparing and Pursing My Career Without College*

I finally landed a job in Charlotte working for a company that owned and operated theatres all over the state of North Carolina. It was just minimun wage; but it was a job. I soon earned enough money and saved enough to buy myself a car and then purchased a used mobile home. Me at the early age of 18-19 years of age buying a mobile home and all the responsibilities of paying bills. Why?, my goodness, I knew nothing about paying bills and getting groceries for myself, but I soon learned. I was just excited to be out on my own and away from the dark secrets that was so embedded within my mind and soul. I had at that time a horrible child-hood and things happened to me that I can scarelessly talk about. I went many, many years not talking to anyone about my childhood and things that happened to me. I will say this; I would not have wanted my daughter to go through the things that I had to go through. Being so young and vunurable was an act of lawlessness on my sister's part. After I had landed my good job in Charlotte; it was not long after that that I soon received word from the home place that my father had passed away with a massive heart attack. So, here I am living out on my own and getting this kind of news from home. I barely knew my father because it felt like I had been away from home for so long . . . . I had left after mother was killed in the train accident. So, I was just devistated, All I could think about was, "why did I not move back home with him"?, I could have taken good care of him. I mean after all, I loved my father. Those thoughts went through my mind many, many nights. I wanted to move home; but I didn't want to lose my friends down south. My high school friends, my acquaintances I had met. I would miss everyone—but all I did at that time was talk about it and never moved or acted upon anything. Well, I lived in that mobile home for just a few years, maybe one or two and soon sold it. Again, I was lonely, sad, distraught, scare, and all the other things that fall into the category of "being young and on your own".

After I gathered my belonging and had things packed up (which was very little), I moved back to West Virginia for good. Up the interstate, moving along at a high rate of speed, all I could think about was "finally home" and it was home. You know the sister I shared earlier about moving in with one of the older ones that had gotten a divorce and had the two children. Well, the sis that moved in with her had gotten married and moved to Summersville, West Virginia—so again, I moved in with her and her two children to try and get back on my feet again. I lived with them for a short while; landed me a job up at the airport in Charleston, West Virginia working for Hertz-Rent-A-Car. I loved that job—they flew me to Dulles-International Airport for training on how to become a representative for the company and I was feeling pretty good about myself by this time. Here I am; with no college education and had this nice job offer and felt like a million dollars. They supplied me with a uniform, yellow and black in color. I had black pants, yellow shirts and yellow sweathers. I was really excited about that job. I loved working there; never in my wildest dreams, I never knew that I would meet the man that I would marry right there at that airport located on the mountaintop in Charleston, West Virginia. After working there for a few short months, I managed to purchase another mobile home over in Kanawha City. It's amazing, I had gotten involved in church where my sister and her children went and little did I know that Jesus had someone at that airport on that mountaintop . . . . I would soon fall in love and so I did, I met this guy who came into my life named Bruce and he also worked up on that mountaintop at the airport. In fact, he worked for United Airlines, so did his father—they both worked for United Airlines.

Now, this was the real deal; I had met this nice guy, he was nice to me and he cared for me. Finally in my life, I had met someone who cared for me, I can recall him sending me a dozen of roses on the job. He was truly a gentleman; wonderful person and still is to this day. I'm sure you have heard people say many times . . . . well, ya know God has somebody for everybody and ya know what?, that's true. We began to date and was courting him on a regular basis. Now I have never been one to live alone and did not like it at all; but I had to do what I had to do. I worked second shift at the airport working the hours of three to eleven at night. I was coming home from work one night and someone had followed me, broke into the front door and I managed to escape out the back door, so I sold I had sold my mobile home in Kanawha City and moved in with a girl-friend who worked with me at the airport for Hertz. She had a place up in South Hills way, way up on top of a mountain there in

Charleston. I remember I slept in a room that had nothing but windows and boy was it cold in that place. My friend was raising a child by herself, so she barely had enough money to pay for electric—much less food. I payed her a little money to stay there until I had gotten so sick from sleeping out in that room with no heat—that my tonsils had gotten infected.

# Chapter 13

## *God Sent Bruce To Love Me*

I was still dating this guy named Bruce and I remember he bought me a pair of shoes to wear to work, because when I met him all I was wearing was a pair of sandles to work. He bought me a coat, boots, gloves and plenty of stuff for Christmas one year. I met the man that I knew would take care of me for the rest of my life. I remember going to his house and his mother took me up to the doctor and they told me that my throat was so infected, that I was going to be out of work for sometime in order for the infection to go away. So, his mother took me back and forth to the doctor and she nursed me back to health. She was the sweetest woman that I know of and is still that way today. Now at this doctor's office, he was giving me of shots of antibiotic medicine to clear up the infection in my body. It was not long after that, maybe a couple of months that Bruce had talked with his parents about me moving in with them. Well, they had a small single size bed up front of the house. They said it would be fine for me to move in there. So there I stayed until we saw what the future would hold for the both of us; but I knew the day would come when I would have to tell him about my "high-school years and the abuse I had went through.

So, we soon began looking at rings and sure enough—he purchased me a diamond ring and we both found our way headed to the altar to get married. So, with onlookers from family and friends on both sides; we were married in a small church up Campbells Creek, West Virginia. We had a nice small wedding, and of course, not having any financial help from family, I was on my own as far as expenses. Bruce helped me pay for a lot of things because I never would have been able to pay for what I thought were the simplest things in life "which was my wedding", had it not been for him. I had my wedding dress made by a young woman that lived in Charleston, West Virginia. I think the material cost me about ten dollars and I had to pay the woman for making it, which at that time I think was about twenty dollars. We had our wedding, repeated our wedding vows before God and family. It was a quiet, but small wedding. We left shortly after the wedding on our honeymoon to Myrtle Beach, South

Carolina. We were both very happy and in love—from two people who met at the airport on a mountaintop overlooking Charleston, West Virginia.

Well, we weren't married long, living in a mobile home that Bruce had bought for us to live together after we go home from our honeymoon. We were both working at the airport and soon I found myself without a job. I cannot remember what went wrong or what happened with that job, probably left on my own accord. So now, we have been married for five months and still knew things were not right with me or anything about me for that matter. I felt there was something missing and longed for but could not put my finger on what it was. We were married in the month of April, 1979—so from that month until the fall of the year, September, 1979 I will still searching for the void in my life. I made a phone call to a sister that was living in the same state; but it was about an hour or so drive to her home. I spoke with her briefly about what type of feelings I was having and she invited Bruce and I up to her home that evening. After the phone call had ended with my sister on the other end; I walked across that mobile home floor; picked up the phone again and called Bruce at work. I was crying and told him that things were not right in our marriage. Now, he did not understand at the time what I was even talking about, but I said on the other end of that phone line "we are going to have to talk when you get home". Well, we did and I told him that I had spoke to a sister of mine who had invited us up to her house. All the way there, Bruce keep saying—what are we going there for?, . . . 'I told him I could not figure it out either'; but that I knew there was a void in my life and that my sister was going to invite her pastor over to her home. Soon her pastor arrived and I explained to him the feelings I was having and I remember that pastor saying to me "it's Jesus tugging at your heart" and that's the emptyness I was feeling. I wanted to know about this Jesus that my mother used to talk about all the time. I felt this tugging at my heart and knew we would have a happy marriage if we both got involved in church and gave our life to Christ. "If we confess our sins, he is faithful and just to forgive us our sins and cleanse us from all unrighteousness" . . . I John 1:9—So right there in her living room—Bruce and I fell to our knees; confessed our sins before God—repeated the sinner's prayer and God saved Bruce and I both. Our life had been changed and immediately we got involved in our local church. After much consideration, we joined Elkview Baptist Church in Elkview, West Virginia—not too far from our house. We got involved there with the Sunday School program; attended every worship service. Things were still not right, so we spoke to our pastor there at the church and he said . . . . 'have you both been baptized' and we said "no". Well, we followed in "Believers Baptism" at that church and became members of that body of believers. We started growing in the Lord, reading His word and soon we were just like what my mother talked about and lived by daily in her own life.

# Chapter 14

## *God Blesses Us With Our Only Son*

After living there in that mobile home court for about three years, I found out that I was pregnant with my first child. Little did I know that I would only carry that child for three months and had a mis-carriage. That happened in June of 1981. Then in September of the same year; I conceived another child and was able to carry him a full term. Now, not having a mother at home to go to with the help of having a baby; not able to tell her my hurts, my pains of childbirth . . . I felt at that point, what am I going to do? I am having a baby and I know nothing about babies. So, in June of 1982 the sweetest baby boy arrived in our home and we deciced we would name this boy, "Brian". I had the "baby blues" really bad and thought to myself—what are we going to do with this baby? He cries all the time, he seems to not like us. Here we are, young new parents and I certainly didn't know anything about tending to babies. So, after being home about one week or so, I called back to the hospital and told them that my baby continues to cry. The nurse on the other line says and I can remember this like it was yesterday, "are you loving your baby"? What in the world did she mean by that?, I thought. On the other end of that telephone line this nurse lady tells me to hold my baby tight and let it feel love from me.

Well, sure enough that worked and from then on—I loved on my baby boy. Not having a mother, I had no clue what to do, so it was truly a trial and error for Bruce and I. We had our baby Brian in church and not long after that we had a ceremony at church where we would have him dedicated to the Lord. The pastor met with us and we told him that we wanted to bring Brian up in the church and teach him the values of christian living and about Jesus. And, so we did—up until the age of eighteen year old when he left home we kept him in church. He was involved in the Awana program there at Elkview Baptist Church and at the age of four years old; we moved south. Bruce and I both had jobs in Charlotte, North Carolina. I was working at Presbyterian Hospital in the lab and he was working part-time at Piedmont Airlines. We weren't here long until we found us a church in Denver called Denver Baptist Church and little did we know the pastor was a guy that I had went to high school with. We moved our membership from Elkview Baptist to Denver Baptist and there we became involved in all activities. We worked in the nursery, sang in the choir and other things. Bruce became active deacon in the church and was responsible for families that were under him. It was a small church; but we loved the people and were loved on by the people. We seen hard times financially and many times the members took up love offerings and gave them to us to help us out. Bruce had quit his job at Piedmont Airlines because it was only part-time and considering the distance from Denver to Charlotte was just too far. He landed a job at this construction company in Lincolnton, North Carolina. When it rained; he would not work, so there was never any pay for that day and if it rained for a week; well no pay for the week. Times were hard, but Jesus met our every need. He took care of us through it all. We grew to love a lot of members at Denver Baptist Church. I have still maintained friendships with many of the ladies and I will also go on to mention that these ladies made a hugh impact on my life because of their testimony and their christian walk they had with God. So, I have the real pleasure to mention a few by name . . . Mrs. Sandy Borders; Mr. Karen Cloninger; Mrs. Carolyn Ratcliff; Mrs. Sue Thom; Mrs.

Suzanne Bigham . . . . (all who gave me plenty of spiritual guidance) during hard times in my life. They prayed with me on many ocassions and I know without a doubt God put these ladies in my life just for the purpose of helping me cope with the difficulties the scars left on my life. I found myself just the other day speaking with my dear friend Karen Cloninger, whom I have grown to love, about various things in my life and how understanding she was and the godly counsel. What an amazing woman! She's so understanding on many things . . . I remember the day she shared with the church the doctor had diagnosed her with cancer and many times when you think a person would be down—well, not Karen Cloninger, why, she was lifting people up. So, not only was she a christian, but someone whom you could go to for advice and/or she would just give me a pat on the back and say "I love you more". I also find Sandy Borders to be of good christian values, a close friend whom I feel could go to with just about anything and discuss situations that occur on a daily basis and she would be faithful, taking time to listen. Sometimes, that's all it takes is someone to listen. Folks, it's true in the Bible where it says "A man who has friends must himself be friendly, But there is a friend who sticks closer than a brother" . . . . Proverbs 18:24. I truly love my dear friends in Christ.

I remember a time sitting in church on a Wednesday night, carrying a heavy burden on my heart from a close family member. I had shared with Carolyn Ratcliff after church the things that were bothering me and I remember her saying to me . . . "well, let's just pray right now and so we did". I have had these ladies have prayer with me on the telephone before and you can just feel the love they have for you. Special people!!!

We soon enrolled Brian in some local sports that is associated with the optimist club program. He played with the pee-wee football team and softball team. The T-ball team is what he started out with first and moved from that league into the older softball programs. He was involved in these sports and Bruce coached one of the teams. Every Saturday we would head out to the ball games and stay just about all day. We met lots of people and was involved in the community and our local church. Everybody knew who Brian Arnold was because he was so out-going and he had a great personality. He not only went to church; but he helped with backyard bible schools during the summer, doing whatever anybody ask him to do. He went every year on youth trips with the youth group of the church. We loved Brian so much and keep him involved in as much activities at school and church that he didn't have time to think about anything else much. He went with his father on adult mission trips (one in particular that I recall was Osage Beach, Missouri). That was a life changing experience for both of them. They came back from that trip and Bruce was a changed man. His life was turned upside down in many good ways and I will share one particular story with you. He was never getting to work with this construction company much; so he prayed while out on the mission trip that God would lead him to a different company. Well, God did. He applied for a position at this company that required lots of testing. He passed all the tests and landed the job that he has now. He was hired in sixteen years ago as general labor in the manufacturing plant. He has worked his way up the "ladder" from supervisor to now "assistant manager". He worked nights on third shift; he worked second shift as supervisor and now works day shift, Monday through Friday. All things work together for good to those who are called according to the purpose of God. Bruce still talks about that mission trip out there in Missouri. Since then, they have gone on other mission trips all over the United States. Our church is all about mission work and the Baptist Men get together and get these teams and go all over. They sacrifice their vacation time and family time to do mission work for God and the people living in the communities.

We had wonderful fond memories of our son Brian. I remember when we bought his first bicycle for Christmas. He took it outside to learn how to ride his bike and was so excited about it . . . . his daddy was holding the back end of it at the seat and Brian would say . . . . "dad, just don't let go, okay". Now, little did he know, he was riding that bike just shortly after his daddy let go and away he went. Didn't take him long to learn how to ride a bike. He was very active in sports and such starting early in his years of life. He started playing "t-ball" around the age of 4 or 5 and sports became a big part of his life. He played varsity football and basketball in high school. I remember when he made the basketball team; he called home and said 'dad , , , , hey dad . . . guess what?, I made the team, oh I made the team. Oh the excitement in his voice on the other end of that telephone was something else. Brian had football practice in the evening after school and his daddy was there for every practice . . . standing by the fence yelling for him to play hard. His dad never missed a practice and never missed a game. He took drivers education in school and soon had his drivers license at the age of 16. One late evening after a high school football game, he was coming home and his car broke down on the side of the road. We always made sure he had a cell phone with him and I can remember him calling late that night (around 12:00pm) and he said, "dad, my car is broken down" . . . his daddy said, "son, don't worry—I'm on my way". Brian spoke back to his dad . . . . "dad, please hurry". Well, it was pitch dark outside, no traffic on the road to speak of much and it was right frightful to be broken down on the side of the road. Especially in this day and age, no one wants to be broken down in a car, flat-tire or anything else for that matter, right? Well, we travelled all over to the middle schools and high schools for his games. Not only did his daddy cheer him on; but he also video tapped his games, of which we still have. His sports kept us busy and that we liked because every Friday night we knew where we were going and there was no questions to that at all. Not only did his sports keep him busy; but he was also inducted into the Beta Club in high school and that was such an honor. I kept every report card he ever got, I kept just about everything he ever made for us in school. I have valentine cards that he made for us in school. I can remember now . . . words like "I love you mommy" written on the cards. What a cherished item, along with many other things he made for me which I have kept and will pass down to my grand-daughter when she gets older.

# Chapter 15

## *Effects of the Empty Nest*

So now, 18 years had gone by and he went off to college. How the empty-nest syndrome causes pain for everybody that has children gone off to college and away from home for the very first time, I'll explain how I felt. It came to me as a shock and I was not prepared for this at all. I mean after all, I only had 18 years to prepare myself for the day when he was going to leave home and go to college, but anyhow I experienced it with such emotions and can remember boo-hoo'ing all the way home when we dropped him off on that college campus yard. Our son was was very intelligent for for that very reason, he was awarded the Presidental Scholarship which helped pay for some of his college tuition every year in college. He was beginning to move on with his life; meeting up with new friends. The old school years had passed away and new things were beginning to take shape in his life. But, what now for my life? Back at home, I beginning to feel and taste the "empty-nest symdrome" that I had heard other mothers talk about so frequently when their children went off to school. I remember driving him to Boiling Springs where the University was located which he was going to attend for 4+ years. It seems like it took hours to get there from his home, but it only took one hour to come home . . . . My oh my, I cried and cried for days and even now wish I would have tried to have more children. That is the biggest regret in my life and if I could do it all over again, I would have tired and tired until I had a daughter. Ya see, little did we know our son would some day meet a young lady right there at the college campus, fall in love with her and get married. So, indeed he did. In is freshman year of college, he met a young lady named Tracy. Two years had passed and he bought her an engagement ring and to our surprise; they set their date to be married in the month of June; so in the year of 2004; they were married on the campus of Gardner Webb University in the chapel where they met. They both went back to college in the fall of 2004; received their Masters Degree—hers in Nursing and his in Christian Education and Counseling. They are presently living in Shelby, North Carolina and have purchased their first home in a quiet neighborhood.

Brian is serving as a youth pastor in full-time service at their local church. Every year he takes his youth group on mission trips within the United States and stays active with his youth. They have local car washes and other events to raise support for the youth to go on their trips. I can honestly say he puts everything into his position as youth pastor; overseeing his youth group, being there for each one of them. God has blessed him with the gift of listening and believe me when I say this . . . . there are so many youth out there with many problems of their own. He patiently listens to their hurts; if any member of his youth ends up in the hospital for any reason, whether late or not, off he would go to visit and have prayer with them. Brian has a hugh heart for young people and desires to see them all achieve spiritually and academically in school. He is there for the young people in the community.

I knew time would permit and I would have the opportunity to share with Bruce and Brian some tough times I endured had when my mother was killed along with other things that happened in my life growing up as his mother and as a wife to my husband. I had never opened up to either one of them and carried this silence within my heart for many years. Brian had been married for about a year now and I can remember him coming home one weekend by himself and he says to me . . . "mom, right there if the person you need to be loving on" and pointed to his father. I broke down in tears and shared with the both of them something that had happened to me when I was 14 years old. My son took it extremely hard and showed a lot of emotions after sharing with him what had happened and things that took place in my life after my mother was killed. They both suggested that I seek out godly counsel to try and help me to deal with the pain and suffering I had gone through. So, after months had gone by . . . I decided in my best interest they were right and through a friend at Denver Baptist Church, she recommended a Christian Counseling Service located close-by; so I made the phone call and told them that I needed someone to talk with. How does a person go to anybody and talk to them about their worse "nightmares"; sit down and talk one on one with professional counsel? Little did I know, I found myself sitting in her office sharing my deepest thoughts from my childhood up; losing my mother at the mere age of 14 years old in a horrific train accident that left the whole family paralyzed; managed to leave home from my older siblings and father to live with an older sister and her husband at their request and ended up at the end of the road, literally.

I counseled with the counseling service for many months and was able to realize there was hope beyond tragic things that happen in a person's life. She suggested different books for me to read; purchased them and continued with my counsel—sometimes going 2-3 times per week at first. It was finally out in the open the horrible life I had to lead when my mother was killed and on into my adulthood life. It was such a blessing that God opened the doors and allowed me to share my inner thoughts with this christian woman who owned and operated Christian Counseling Service locally. What a great relief to be able to sit and talk with someone that I knew would not "gossip" all over town my personal life with people that I knew. So, to all the people out there who have suffered great loss, whether it be from a loved one passing away, losing a child or what-ever the case maybe, there is Hope and YOU CAN easily pick yourself up and move along your journey in this life for what God has called us here on this earth to do. It's never ever too late to seek out counsel or find that close friend to share your hurting past with.

# Chapter 16

## *Our First Grand-Daughter Is Born*

So, now my son and his wife have been married for 7 years and just recently surprised us with a beautiful grand-daughter and they named her "Addison Grace". This little princess was born on May 1, 2010; and literally has brought so much joy in my life. Was this the little girl that I wished I could have had when I was in my younger years? Oh my goodness, looking back over our son's birth and toddler stages; his daughter looks exactly like he did and it's like re-living those stages all over again. Here she is with "blond hair" and "blue eyes" . . . the prettiest child we've seen in a long time. My personal goals are to be the best grandmother I can be to her. My husband feels the same way about her—we just love our "baby Addison". When I have the opportunity to be with her; I will always live an example of a godly christian grand-mother and feel that this would have a great impact on her life even if I don't get to see her often. I am praying now that Addison will come to know Christ at an early young age; keeping faith that God will mature her into a lovely christian lady who was born to honor God and seek out his commandments for her life and to see souls saved for His kingdom.

Everything we try to accomplish in life comes on the wings of Faith. I have an angel around the rear view mirror in my car with these words written on it, FAITH . . . It reminds me every day to keep faith in God and He will sustain every aspect of my being, regardless of how much I have to go through in my own life and have been through in my life; knowing I will always have trials that come my way. I heard a pastor in Texas say these things about faith: There's Natural Faith; Little Faith; Mustard Faith, Great Faith; Measure of Faith; Faithless Faith and Visible Faith. He mentioned "Natural Faith" as having the faith that the other driver in the lane will not come into my lane causing a head-on collision or the co-pilot of an airplane knows the difference from Miami to Chicago. "Little Faith" as a person needs just little faith to get by in this life on. "Mustard Faith" as having this much faith that we could move mountains. "Great Faith" as having great faith we have in our Lord. "Measure of Faith" as a small amount of faith needed to accomplish His will. "Faithless

Faith" as not having any faith at all, in anything. "Visible Faith" as you see things happening in one's life . . . i.e. healing or through sickness. Just a few things to think about as I feel and sense the real meaning of Faith.

I have had plenty to talk about growing up as a child and now I myself am getting older. The older one gets, the more closer they are to reaching their heavenly home. I've heard many preachers say . . ."Mr. and/or Mrs . . . , so and so . . . where do you live?, and where's your home? To their reply, they would say, well, I live on such and such a street in such and such a town; but my home is in heaven. There's not a sweeter word under my breath than "heaven" and as I have matured and gotten older I ponder what heaven is going to be like. In the Bible, there is a book of Revelation—it plainly identifies what heaven is going to look like and you know, if my son out lives me; he will one day have to make those same decisions that we made so many years back on my mother. It's a peaceful thought to encounter to know where a person will go when they leave this world and thank God I made that decision about my life back in September, 1979.

I will finish this book in hopes that I will always so love God first; put others first in my life; and always so love my daughter-in-law, Tracy, in spite of the failures that come my way. I pray that God always allows me to be more involved with her so we will have a better relationship with each other in the many years to come. As of this date; we have not been able to develop a close, loving, God-centered relationship and I could not possibly tell you what her likes and dis-likes are.; but one thing for sure . . . I do understand with God all things are possible and I do pray that God removes all distractions and hurtles in our life so that we may love one another the way God says in his word "This I command that you . . . . Love One Another". Someday God will give us the opportunity to do so and this I have the faith to believe in.

I so love my grand-daughter, Addison, with all my heart. I pray that God always directs her paths as she matures in Him, in such a crazy mixed-up world out there. I remember the day she was born and how emotional my son was when he swung open the doors on that maternity ward floor and said . . . she's here! He picked me up off the floor, swung me around . . . he was so happy, proud and emotional, cried with his arms wrapped around me and whispered these words "mom, I'm a daddy". I will never forget that as long as I live on this earth. I pray Addison gets the real privilege of getting to know "me" as her grandmother and her "pop" as her grandfather. (our son's side of the family). I hope she always stay true to who she is and doesn't put on aires for anybody. I pray she puts Christ first in her life, prays about everything first and studies His word and hides it in her heart. She's so beautiful, "Addison" grama loves you darling!!!

I so love my son, Brian with all my heart. He's the only child we had and in looking back now, I wish we could have had more children, but it was not in His plan for our lives. I pray that Brian will always walks close to God and finds comfort in knowing Him calling on Him for his every need. Thank you Brian for making us proud. You've obeyed His call into the ministry and we love you son. I'm glad that God gave you to me for just a short period of time. I'm am so honored to be your mother!

And lastly, I so love my husband Bruce. My struggles have been hard to bare; but you have stuck by me through it all, comforted me and was so understanding so many times in the 32 years of our marriage. ~ "I love you honey" ~ Thanks for being who you are, and because of who you are . . . . you are . . . . loved by so many! You would do without, so others could have and I have seen that demonstrated in your life so many times.

**—The End**

Brothers, from left to right front row:
Vernon, John, Paul and Roy
back row: Mike, Martin and Sam

Sisters, from left to right ront row:
Mary, Leah, Doris and Martha
back row: Becky, Veronica, Janice and Evelyn

May God bless each and every one of you as you read this book and I hope you find the sense of hope I found in 1979 when I gave my heart and life to Christ. I never dreamed I would have had to go through many things; but God was with me through it all. To God Be The Glory; Great Things He Has Done.— . . . . *Veronica Rudd Arnold*